"There is life after downsizing... primer on how to pick yourself up if you've become a victim of the 'new economy.' Don't panic ... take a deep breath and read this book."

— Randy Gorbman
Host/Producer: *The Western New York Business Report*
WHAM Radio, Rochester, NY

"Bill has hit a homerun! *The One Hour Survival Guide for the Downsized* is full of practical wisdom and business sense that the average person can use right now. What a pleasure to read. My brain is going a million miles per second applying these dynamic principals. Thanks Bill Tatro for writing this very timely 'book of wisdom.'"

— Dr. Joseph M. Burress
Pastor
Victory Baptist Church, Rochester, NY

"Having some two decades in the business of outplacement work, I really appreciate the effort put into this book. Downsizing is no fun for anyone. Tatro takes a serious look at a problem that hundreds of thousands of Americans are facing and offers positive solutions."

— Emory W. Mulling
Chairman, The Mulling Companies
Author, *The Mulling Factor: Get Your Life Back by Taking Control of Your Career*

"When times are tough, it is important to have guidance that is realistic and understandable. That is exactly what this book provides its readers."

— **Lewis Losoncy, Ed.D.**
The Doctor of Encouragement
Author, ***If It Weren't For You, We Could Get Along: How to Stop Blaming and Start Living***

"Downsizing can be a rough time in anyone's life. This is truly a survival guide that can be read in an hour and put to immediate use. Congratulations on a job well done."

— **Carol Hacker**
Carol A. Hacker & Associates
Author, ***How to Compete in the War for Talent: A Guide to Hiring the Best***

The One Hour Survival Guide for the Downsized

What You Need to Know When You're Let Go

The One Hour Survival Guide for the Downsized

What You Need to Know

When You're Let Go

by

William L. Tatro, IV

PRESS

A Division of the Diogenes Consortium
SANFORD • FLORIDA

© 2002 William Tatro
All Rights Reserved.

All rights reserved. No part of this publication may be reproduced, stored in a retrieval system, or transmitted in any form or by any means — electronic, mechanical, photocopy, recording, or any other — except for brief quotations in printed and electronic reviews, without the prior permission of the publisher.

Published by DC Press
2445 River Tree Circle
Sanford, FL 32771
http://www.focusonethics.com

This book was set in Adobe Centaur
Cover Design and Composition by Jonathan Pennell

Library of Congress Catalog Number: Applied For
    Tatro, IV. William L.,
The One Hour Survival Guide for The Downsized: What You Need to Know When You're Let Go
    ISBN: 1-932021-00-0

First DC Press Edition
10   9   8   7   6   5   4   3   2
Printed in the United States of America

DEDICATION

To my wife Patricia

who has always been there

and has always believed

ACKNOWLEDGMENTS

SPECIAL THANKS to those who gave great aid, support and at times a shoulder to cry on: Melanie Smith, Jeff Katz, Bob Savage, Gary Hunneyman, Quint, Nici and finally my staff at Eagle Steward.

TABLE OF CONTENTS

About the Author xi
Publisher's Comment xvii

Section One: Could It Really Be Me? 1

Section Two: Downsizing as a Social Phenomenon and the Questions to Ask 9

Section Three: Opportunities Come in Different Forms 79

Section Four: Further Reading 83

Conclusion....................................87
Appendix: Lists................................89
Appendix: Notes...............................103

ABOUT THE AUTHOR

WILLIAM L. TATRO, IV AUTHOR of *The Survival Guide for the Downsized* is a graduate of Alfred University with a degree in Economics. Bill spent five years in the classroom where he taught mathematics. His love of teaching carried over into a new profession called Finance. He yielded to the call of Wall Street where his grandfather had been a stock broker for 57 years. Completing a highly successful career at Prudential Bache, now called Prudential Financial, this Senior Vice President and Chairman Counselor, the highest group at Pru Financial, left in 1991 to form the estate planning firm of

THE ONE HOUR SURVIVAL GUIDE

Eagle Steward Ltd. in Rochester, New York. The unique concept of having all the disciplines of finance, law and accounting under one roof quickly made Eagle Steward Ltd. a household name in Western New York. The firm was formed to solve the problems of clients concerning estate taxes, probate and nursing home costs, and to clarify the bias created by conflicting advice given by attorneys, accountants, bankers, insurance agents and financial advisors. Eagle Steward Ltd. has achieved a position of prominence and success with millions of dollars under management, and over 800 clients in 30 states and several foreign countries. With 30 years of financial experience behind him, and residing for 54 years in Rochester, New York, Bill Tatro is uniquely qualified to write a book that not only deals with the financial sides of downsizing, but the emotional aspects as well. Eastman Kodak, "the big yellow box," started downsizing in 1991 with their first major package. Since that time Xerox,

Bausch & Lomb, Corning and many other major fortune 500 companies have begun the process of implementing the 21st Century strategy called: downsizing. Bill has met with hundreds of people who have had first hand experience of what downsizing means. Most recently, Bill's wife, Patricia, was downsized by the State Board of Continuing Education at BOCES. He is not only qualified to write this book— he is *over* qualified. This book is not only due— it is *over* due!

So you've been laid-off. They used to call it being fired, but today it is more politically correct to be called "down-sized".

You're in denial.

You're numb.

You're angry.

You're confused.

You're sad.

You're afraid.

THE ONE HOUR SURVIVAL GUIDE

Right now you have a choice. You can go and grab all the psychological help books that are on the shelves. You can listen to the talk shows to make you feel good about yourself. You can take the overwhelming feelings of disorientation and fear and allow yourself to go inward. Because, after all, none of this was your fault. It's what you could do, but is it what you should do?

> *It reminds me of the couple who were out for a sunny Saturday afternoon. They took their picnic basket, and decided to have a nice leisurely canoe ride in the calm always placid river. As they floated on the river enjoying their luncheon, the current started picking up— faster, and faster, and faster. After a while, they realized they were no longer in control, and what they heard ahead signaled disaster.........***Niagara Falls!***

Two choices were presented at that moment in time.

The first choice was to ignore and, in fact, deny what was happening.

> *They had their picnic afternoon planned. **No one** told them that Niagara Falls was at the end of this river. It couldn't be there! They could get on a cell phone and talk to people about their troubles. They could commiserate with each other. They could look for emotional support. They could seek professional guidance. They could do all the things that the textbooks say should be done. Having that cell phone could connect them with others, and make them **feel better**.*
>
> *And as they got closer and closer to the edge of Niagara Falls, they realized that **feeling better** wasn't going to save them.*

Their second choice was pretty simple...

> *Take hold of the situation, grab the oars and paddle with everything they had, **and survive**.*

You're at that spot right now. You've been let go. You've been fired. You've been down-sized. You feel out of control. No matter what you call it, it is another phase of your life. What you do from here, from this moment in time, is critical. You've taken the first step. You've purchased *The One Hour Survival Guide for the Down-sized*. Take control of your life. Follow the simple suggestions and illustrations, and make this an opportunity— not a calamity! I wish you all the best!

— **BILL TATRO**

P.S. Row like crazy!!!

PUBLISHER'S COMMENT

CALL IT WHAT YOU WILL, but downsizing by any other name ranks right up there with some of the other most devastating events that could possibly occur in a person's life. We've all heard how traumatic the loss of a spouse or child can be; anyone who has ever sold a house and made a major move understands the stress involved. There are numerous stressful events that could happen in one's life — and none of them something we look forward to, however, the loss of your source of income is one that has ramifications that go way beyond expectations.

THE ONE HOUR SURVIVAL GUIDE

Bill Tatro has taken years of experience working with individuals who have faced downsizing and provides on these pages sensible and concrete recommendations for surviving the turn of events. The phenomena we know as "downsizing" isn't new to American workers. It's been occurring under different names for generations, but it has been in the last decade that the term has been taking on a new and often extremely disturbing identity. While much has been written about the impact of downsizing, there isn't much available for those directly affected to put their hands on that can be used to help them through this often devastating period in their lives. This book is a serious attempt to fill the void that exists and provide reasonable and serious assistance.

With coverage of every conceivable issue that one could possibly face during the days, weeks, and months that follow downsizing, this is truly a "survival guide" that will prove invaluable. If you are facing the ominous task of making it through the minefield that is downsizing, let this guide keep you focused and on target. If you have a friend or relative who is facing this threatening period in their life, this would be a most-appreciated gift.

—**Dennis McClellan**
Publisher

The One Hour Survival Guide for the Downsized

What You Need to Know When You're Let Go

SECTION ONE

Could it Really Be Me?

WHEN SOMEBODY has been downsized the first reaction is to question themselves...

It's **not** my fault!

What did **I** do?

Where did **I** go wrong?

Could **I** have done my job better?

When we start to look inward, there *are* questions that have to be answered, but in today's world, downsizing is the new corporate strategy. *However*, there are those instances when you are the *only one* being let go. If that is the case, this guide is not about you in particular. However, with that said, I don't want to discount, or eliminate, your individual situation. Take **all** the ideas that are in this guide and apply them to yourself, but **first** examine some of the aspects of your situation:

- Has this happened more than one time?
- Is this a continual pattern?
- Are you repeatedly finding yourself starting new jobs, only to see things go wrong, and ultimately it ends up that you're discharged (downsized)?

As Bob came up the steps, he knew she would understand. After all, it's happened before. "Hi honey, I'm home," he said. "I'm in the kitchen Bob," Sylvia answered back.

Downsizing is the new corporate strategy.

"You're home a little early aren't you?" she asked. "Well, not by choice. I've been downsized. But it's not my fault." "How many have been let go?" she asked as she turned off the stove. "Well, so far just me," he answered noting the suitcases by the back door.

"Bob, let me explain something to you. Downsizing is when a company cuts everyone, when a department is laid off, when no one is spared......that's downsizing. In the past two years, you've lost six jobs, and each time you've been the only one let go. Bob, you haven't been downsized, you've lost your job."

As Sylvia picked up her bags and walked through the back door, she turned and said, "I left your dinner on the stove. I'll call you when I get settled."

As Bob heard the car leave the driveway, he thought, it sure is tough being downsized.

If you're seeing a pattern, you are going to have to look inward. You must find out what it is that you're doing that has brought you repeatedly to this particular position. That's a simple statement to make, but it may be the truth, and sometimes simple is better. At this step, good professional counseling could help.

If this is the *first* time that you have found yourself on the short end, after several years of faithful service to your company, and it's **ONLY YOU** losing your job, then there may be some legal aspects that you should be examining.

There may be some legal aspects that you should be examining.

Ask Yourself These Particular Questions, and Then Give Yourself an Honest Answer:

- Do you have a written contract?
- Did your employer breach your written contract?
- Do you have an implied contract?
- Did your employer breach your implied contract?

Breach of contract?

Was there discrimination?

Has there been management retaliation?

When do you engage an attorney?

Your employer may have breached your contract by firing you for no reason. You may find you still have some rights, or maybe some implied promises. Check your employee handbook. It could be a lifesaver at the end.

Was there Discrimination? The Civil Rights Act of 1964 prevents any *kind* of discrimination based on race, color, religion, gender, national origin, marriage or sexual orientation. I urge you to tread carefully. It's easy to claim discrimination, but difficult to prove. Look *carefully* at your individual situation. If you feel you've been discriminated against, make sure that documentation of *each* incident has been established to support your claim.

Is my employer trying to retaliate? You've been vocal at your job. You've been a thorn in management's side. You've been the "hard head case," who's impossible to work with. Any of these things could create a retaliatory situation that makes it easy for the employer to justify getting rid of you.

When documenting the role of the employer, make sure that you substantiate dates, times, and exact incidents.

Build yourself a legal case, or "paper your files" as they say. If, in fact, your employer is doing something illegal, or trying to harm your reputation, *proof* is always going to be paramount. *So, make sure you're loaded with it!*

Now if you've collected this data, and you're the only one who's being let go, what do you do next? **CONSULT AN ATTORNEY**, because at this point in time there may be grounds for a lawsuit — breach of contract, discrimination, retaliation or any similar unfair treatment are causes for legal action.

If in this instance your employer *has singled you out*, remember that if you have a pattern of this happening to you, it's time to look at your own individual history and personality. Who are you? What do you think, and how do those feelings affect your performance on the job? All of this should be taken into account **before** you make accusations! *The problem could be with you!*

However, if it's a first time occurrence, you believe it is unjustified, and if you can prove it, it is time to go into action and get an attorney. Because, *the problem is not with you!*

SECTION TWO

Downsizing as a Social Phenomenon and the Questions to Ask

Downsizing does not treat you as an individual.

DOWNSIZING DOES NOT TREAT YOU as an individual. In other words, you were not taken into consideration in the corporate decision. Downsizing coldly cuts a group, a department, a section, or a whole plant. It's important to understand the *reason* for your termination. Understanding *why* you were let go as part of a group is important in *The One Hour Survival Guide for the Downsized*.

Understand that it's not you! Downsizing is the new corporate strategy of the 21st century. There's nothing you could have done.

"I worked hard, and was there for a long time, I did my job, I was loyal and this is how they treat me!" The natural human reaction is simply to turn away in disgust.

- The company has changed.
- The people have changed.
- They are not who I always thought they were.
- They don't know what they're doing
- It's a bad company.

There's nothing you could have done.

**Well, you're right!
They have changed,
and it
is different!**

It's a new delivery system with technological advancements. There are new products with just in time inventory delivery. There are new ways. It's a new company. But unfortunately, new ways conflict with old feelings and old attitudes. After all, we're human beings.

First and foremost, understand that the reason for your termination is *not you!*

Psychologically that helps you get started on the road to survival.

What's Next? You're going to get a notice that you will have to report for a meeting with your Human Resources Director.

THE ONE HOUR SURVIVAL GUIDE

Oh, that's going to be fun, you think, I'm going to give them all a piece of my mind!

No, you're not!

That would be the dumbest thing in the world, because Human Resources didn't create this situation. They have a job to do. They can't make you feel better. Oh, they may try, but after talking to hundreds of people just like you, it gets old after awhile. Don't make it difficult by going to the meeting with an attitude. You need these people, because H.R. has a lot of the answers and suggestions that might be beneficial

Human Resources didn't create your situation.

Before the Human Resources Meeting:

- Simply inquire if there are other positions in the company that are available to you.

- You may find you have employment options within the company.

- Will the company train you for those new positions?

- If the positions are in a different geographical area, will they pay relocation expenses?

Don't leave the Human Resources meeting with unanswered questions.

The Human Resources Meeting:
You're going to go into that meeting, and while you're sitting there, they'll have a checklist they are going to address — step, by step, by step. Understanding what they're going to ask you, being in a position to make sure that you're clear about what it is *you* need to know, and being knowledgeable about the information that they are *required* to give you is paramount on the road to survival for the downsized.

Don't leave the H.R. meeting with *any* unanswered questions!

So, what is the checklist, and more importantly, what should *you* be asking?

However, before we start making lists, let's look at the PACKAGE. I touch on this briefly because Packages are presented over time and allow you to decide whether you want to stay on. Don't be afraid to use the ideas in this guide even though I'm directing my comments to those who have no choice.

Packages may contain a year's salary, additional education benefits for retraining, continued medical benefits, and even social security bridge plans. Packages are usually discussed at your company. You'll know it well in advance. You will have time to analyze the offer, and see if it is something you want to take.

During the '90's, the packages were coming fast and furious. People had months to make decisions. Now it appears that packages are fewer and are getting smaller, so don't plan on one being offered. The decision to stay or go has

If there is a "package," make sure you completely understand it.

been taken out of your hands. You've been downsized!

The Final Paycheck

It seems a simple thing, but when you are told what the severance pay is, make **sure they have your correct addres**s. If they are going to send you a check or your final W-2, sometimes the mailing address is incorrect, so make sure that it's absolutely 100% accurate. Rightly or wrongly in your mind, the final paycheck or severance pay is the *money you're going to live on immediately.* Understanding **exactly** the amount of money you're going to receive, and over what time period, is critical not only to your pocketbook, but also your emotional well being!

- How much is the severance pay?
- When do I get it?
- Is it over a period of time?
- Is it a lump sum?

What about the last Check?

- When does it end?

So, now you've started the list. Remember you're looking for information. It's your survival so keep your cool.

Next, Insurance Information

- What are you expecting to learn?
- What do you need to know?
- First and foremost, what are you and your family's health benefits?
- Will they be continued?
- Are they portable? (This means can you take them to another company.)

In most instances, you're going to get a Consolidated Omnibus Budget Reconciliation Act letter (COBRA). COBRA allows you to purchase insurance over an extended period of time. You'll have 30 days to decide if you want to pay into a COBRA Health Plan, or buy into a short term medical plan. In most instances, you

COBRA – what is it and how will it impact your life?

Know where you stand in respect to insurance coverage – all insurance.

can continue to remain in the short term plan for up to two years. A family situation or a preexisting condition could dictate the choice. In most instances, for the average family, a savings of several hundred dollars a month could be realized by going with the short plan. Understand what the **exact cost** is going to be, and the **exact length of time** you will be able to operate under COBRA. The worst thing in the world is to feel that you or your loved ones are totally unprotected. Since the cost of health care today is astronomical, it is imperative that you have a clear understanding of exactly what is covered under your health plan and/or COBRA.

- If you have a **dental plan**, will that continue?

Feeling comfortable that you and your family are covered will go a long way during this process.

This is not an expense we can cut, so forget about going without medical insurance. Along with health insurance,

Is there dental coverage?

through the company, you may have been carrying a group term life insurance or disability policy. You need to know the facts about what happens to these policies.

What about life or disability insurance?

- Do you have the opportunity of picking up additional life and disability insurance?

- Is the life and disability insurance portable? Can you take it to the next company?

- If it is **not**, how long does it stay intact?

- Are you covered for a period of time? What kind of relationship has the company developed with the underlying carrier?

Usually companies eliminate life and disability insurance when you are downsized, but we need to know and it doesn't hurt to ask. It's possible that the company can recommend new carriers.

Is there "anything" for which the company owes you reimbursement? Leave no stone unturned.

The List Continues:

- Does the company owe you any money other than your regular salary? I'm referring to traditional vacation days and sick days. This will be another file that the H.R. person will consult.

- What is the company policy?

- How do they pay those sick days and vacation days?

- Will it be paid over a period of time or will it be paid in one final check? Make sure your records and theirs are the same. If there is a disagreement have proof that you are right and the company is wrong.

- You may have some unpaid expenses that came out of your pocket for which you are waiting to be reimbursed. Make sure that your documentation is in order, so that when you go into your H.R. meeting it is clearly understood that you expect

THE ONE HOUR SURVIVAL GUIDE

to be reimbursed. Ask when and how.

- Documentation and proof is the key!

401(K) Information:

The H.R. person will next review your 401(K) information, and will start to explain those options to you. You're doing well. You've maintained your composure (kept your cool). Let's keep going.

I'll discuss later HOW you're going to *use* your 401(K). But listen to the H.R. person explain what options you have.

- Must I take it?

- Can I leave some, or all, in the plan?

- Clarify if there are any penalties for taking a lump sum distribution and rolling it into an IRA.

- Make sure that you have a copy of your most recent statement. It should show **exactly** where your

This is important!

READ CAREFULLY

401(K) is located, and the current value.
- Also, make sure you have a toll free phone number that you can call to directly connect you with the investment house that holds your 401(K).
- If you are entitled to a pension, make sure you understand when it starts, how much it pays, and what the terms are.

If you have a spouse, the Employee Retirement Income Security Act of 1974 (ERISA) rules come into play. Make sure the H.R. person explains all the rules about your spouse signing off on your pension and/or taking partial distributions. Take any written information they offer.

Nearing the end of the H.R. meeting:

If, before going into this closing meeting, you made inquiries about other available positions in the company, I would re-ask if anything new has appeared. Inquire if things start to change at the company, whether you will be notified and have the opportunity of getting your job back. Ask your H.R. person if there are any funds available for continuing education or retraining? It may have been available in a prior package and may **not** be available now.

A simple inquiry as to what the company's policy is never hurts!!

- Finally, can the company do anything for you in seeking other employment?

- Are there resources, or individuals, that can help you write a resume' or assist you in putting one together?

- Can Human Resources direct you to someone who can help, if they can't?

Downsizing is impersonal. The company is practicing new strategies, so don't

Don't Hesitate to ask for help

think that their lack of help is personal. *It is not.* It's almost impossible to individually aid everyone, but ask. Your company may be the exception to the rule. Finally, reconfirm the final paycheck. Is it mailed or do you pick it up at a certain time? It's a small thing, but don't assume anything about your final paycheck. As a matter of fact...

Don't assume anything about the closing process!

These key questions, many that will be covered by the H.R. person and many that seem to be standard operating procedure, are paramount to your survival. The answers to these questions will give you a better handle of where you are, where you've been, and more importantly where you're going!

THE ONE HOUR SURVIVAL GUIDE

You have just left the H.R. office.
You were filled with questions and every question was answered.

Do you feel any better? — No!

In fact, you probably feel worse. Because as you walked out of the H.R. office, more than likely, you felt an isolation that you've never experienced before. This company was your life. It's what you did every day. Now, it's over. People say changes are the most difficult events in our lives. Well, you were just given one major change. Take a deep breath, because now you have information.

Information is the key to *The One Hour Survival Guide for the Downsized*.

You, just you, OK ... and your spouse, too!
Now I want you to do something for yourself. Whether it's going out to dinner, seeing a movie, taking a trip, buying something, do something special just for you. This is your reward. You got your infor-

mation, and now you're on the way to survival. Come on and treat yourself to something nice — you deserve it! There! That felt good. Didn't it?

Now it's time to get down to business.
You've got to keep rowing, keep pulling on those oars.

Lists can save your life. Make them, maintain them, and stay on top of them.

Now it's list time.
The first lists you are going to make are going to lay out your **total assets**. They are the positive lists, the feel good lists. These lists compile *everything* you own. On the Non Qualified, Personal, and Qualified Asset **(List #1; pp. 91-94)** included at the end of the guide you record such things as your house, car, CD's, stocks, and bonds. Your 401Ks, IRAs, anything that's collectable, and the cash value of your life insurance — *everything!* I want you to put in front of you everything that you've accumulated over your lifetime. It's yours. It's what your work has accomplished; no

matter how large, no matter how small. Everything tangible has a price tag, so list it. Look at it. See it. This is what you're going to work with.

The next list will detail what you owe — the **liabilities** list (**List #2; p. 95**). They are not such feel good lists, but that's okay, you can deal with it. On these lists will be your mortgage, car payment, home equity loan, credit cards, or any loans from friends — *everything!* Check lists for you to use and fill in are provided.

Assets - liabilities = net worth

This is what you're worth on paper. If you sold everything and were handed a check, your assets minus liabilities would be listed on that check. Most people aren't aware of how much they are worth. They have never taken the time to look. Now you do have time, because you have been ***downsized***. Sit down, make those lists, and determine exactly your **net worth**. It could take

What are

you worth?

a little time to pull all this data together, but right now you have time.

The next list I want you to make is your income list. **Income** is money you're going to receive. It may be in a lump sum, or periodic payments. However you expect to receive it, list it. Your H.R. person already gave you information about your pension, severance pay, vacation pay, and even sick day reimbursements. List everything **(List #3; pp. 96-98)**. You may even qualify for Social Security. You may have rental property. Your cousin Charlie may owe you money and may have been paying you over a period of time. List everything, and list its duration. Once again, a checklist has been provided as a guide for you to utilize.

Finally, I want you to prepare the Personal Budget Expenditures List **(List #4; pp. 99, 100)**. On this current expense list include what you must pay out every month. *Must pay out* does **not** mean the annual trip for skiing, that's ***not a must***. It's nice, but it's not a must. It means utilities, mortgage payments, car payments, credit card payments, anything that is a fixed expense on an ongoing basis. I would be remiss if I didn't say, once again, this form has been provided for you to fill out. Some people call a current expense list a budget, but a budget is something that's been sculpted. We're not going to do that. This simply is what you **must** pay. These are the 'can't live withouts' — "Ok, I'll let you have cable."

What do you do when your lists don't match?

Comparison:

Did I say that we were finished with lists? NOT QUITE YET! There is another list that you are going to create. It's your comparison list of what is coming in versus what is going out **(List #5; p. 101)**. It's simple and it's little. Unfortunately, *it doesn't match*. That's when the panic first hits.

Through the years I've asked husbands and wives, "Do you know for certain that if either of you were to pass away that there would be sufficient assets for your spouse?". Invariably, I would get the answer, "I think so". Well, I think so and know so are miles apart! In this evaluation thinking and knowing are two different things.

Those people didn't have to deal with it until sometime in the future. To them it was just a theoretical question. But for you, it's not theory, it's reality. Because you've been downsized, the future is now. We want to know exactly what's coming in, and exactly what's going out. And now we find that there is a shortfall. You do your lists several times, and all of a sudden it starts to hit home that you're out of a job. Now we are getting to the hard cruel reality that things have changed. We have to start pulling on those oars harder. Our questions were answered by H.R. So, we have the information. Those assets are going to help us get through this.

It's time to reshuffle the deck and get creative!

The first asset we want to look at is the 401(k). Whether it's a little or a lot, it's available to us right now. And yes, I know you might be under 59 ½. Specific rules come into play in a 401(k). This asset has never been taxed. Even though we have accessibility to our 401(k) it is subject to income tax. What about the dreaded penalty? You may be able to leave the 401(k) with the company. If you're between 55 and 60 that may be advantageous. 401(k)s allow 55 to 60-year olds to withdraw penalty free, if they retired or were downsized after age 55, but alas, not tax free. More than likely you are going to remove all of your money from the 401(k).

401(k)

is key!

"I'm not going to leave my money at a company that downsized me," you say,

"I want out!"

The problem is that under 59 ½, if you want your money out of the company's 401(k) and you want to have access to the money, you must have been downsized after age 55, or you must pay a penalty of 10%. Not my penalty; not the company's penalty, the government's. Sorry!

The strategy would be to rollover the 401(k) into an IRA. So, move everything to the IRA...

ONCE IN THE IRA, CAN A 10% PENALTY BE AVOIDED?

Yes! We use what's called a 72T. Equal distributions that can go on for 5 years, or to age 59 $\frac{1}{2}$, whichever is longer. If you start this at age 56 you **can not** stop it at 59 $\frac{1}{2}$, because that is only 3 $\frac{1}{2}$ years. You must continue the 72T until age 61, which will equal the required 5 years. If you are 45, you must continue equal distributions until 59 $\frac{1}{2}$. Be careful, you have to take the **exact** amount each month. No more, no less. Unless you've set up inflation provisions, all increases or decreases of distributions result in all prior distributions paying a 10% penalty.

The smartest thing may be to swallow your pride and leave a portion at the company. (Pride has no nutritional value. Remember, this is survival.) Now, I say a portion, because the choices of where that money can be invested may be limited. The strategy of leaving *some* money at the 401(k), if allowed, and rolling *some* into your IRA, may be the best strategy.

So, now you have a way to access your retirement money. Feeling better?

Property:

One of the biggest assets most people have is their home. When a person has been downsized, the home can present positive and negative factors. It is positive if you have the asset. You own it; it's yours; you have built up equity. The negative is that if you have a mortgage you may not be able to continue paying that mortgage.

Is your house a + or a —?

Deal with the positive first — after all, you're rowing here!

There has been equity built up in your home. A home equity loan may allow you to tap into the increased value. Through refinancing the mortgage, you may be able to remove some or all of what you built up through the years. In addition, by refinancing, you may be able to dramatically reduce your monthly payment. It's worth a look! This is survival, but be careful, because the home is one asset that represents the "American Dream". I like refinancing to cut payments, but the last resort is to take out equity. Knowing how much you have and how much is available is important. Remember, I said knowledge is the most critical element in *The One Hour Survival Guide for the Downsized.* The house is an asset. You may use it.

Insurance:

You may have some type of insurance policy, usually through the company. In the H.R. meeting you learned that insurance usually disappears with downsizing. However, you may have acquired whole life policies over the years, or universal life policies, or even variable universal life policies. Term insurance isn't going to help in this situation. Determine the cash values of these policies, the accessibility of the cash, and whether you still need the insurance. If you're sitting with whole life policies, analyze replacing whole life with variable universal life. This could create the same type of insurance coverage, but allow you access to the cash build up. This strategy could create a tax free cash flow over a period of time, and still keep the overriding insurance in place. Remember, insurance cash value is an asset. You need every asset you have to survive. *Nothing is sacred.*

Is there cash available in your insurance?

Are you liquid?

Investments:

You've got CD's. You've got stocks. You've got bonds. You never wanted to liquidate them until sometime in the future. Well, the future is now, and those particular assets have value. What are they worth? How easily could you liquidate them? Are there back-end penalties? Are there tax implications if you were to liquidate these CD's, stocks, bonds, and annuities that you've been building up? I talked earlier about reshuffling the deck, well now it's time to do it. These assets must create income, cash-flow, and perhaps next month's mortgage payment — **SURVIVAL!** Call the companies. Find out the penalties of getting that money, the steps needed for withdrawal, and request any necessary forms.

Putting it Together and Into Action:

Once you've put together these specific pots of money, your 401(k), equity in the house, insurance policies, investments, and cash, total everything to see what you are working with. Now stop. Put down your pencil, and take a break. You've learned more so far than you ever thought possible. Congratulations, you are on the way to surviving this downsizing!

The break-time is over. It's now time to study your lifestyle. Go back to your expense list. Most people, when they first take a look at the expense list, go at it with a *meat cleaver*. They *chop* this and that, and ultimately **slash lifestyles**. You've been **traumatized** enough. You've been **downsized**, and it's time to put the meat cleaver aside and **take out the scalpel** to do some *fine tuning*. *Discuss with your spouse, every one of your expenses!*

By the way, I just brought your spouse into the discussion. Communication with your loved ones is absolutely paramount. But, in the discussion with your spouse, look together at places where you can trim or cut back.

You CAN survive this thing called "downsizing!"

Communication is the one tool that should never be downplayed.

Communication is your key to success.

Keep the doors of communication open — to your spouse, your former employer, your advisors, to those to whom you owe money.

Example: *If you go out to dinner two or three times a month, keep the number the same, but look for specials, coupons, and give-a-ways.* ***Or****, if you like to rent videos, some places rent the new hits for $3.00, while others rent older hits for $1.00. So, pick some of the movies you haven't seen before, and save 66%.*

Ask yourself, what's *really* important, and get creative! If you like to wash your car every week for $7.00 or $8.00, it's time to get out the bucket and the hose, and do it yourself. You see, every dollar is important, and *every* dollar counts! Start to look at that budget. Look at where it can be tweaked. It's smart today to enhance your energy efficiency by turning off lights, checking your hot water tank, and your air conditioning. Every expense should be scrutinized, but not with a meat cleaver, with a scalpel.

Grocery shopping: Never used coupons before? It's time to start! Go through the magazines and newspapers, and start to clip coupons. Send for rebates and experience bulk shopping. You may have to buy a few more cans of tuna fish, but the savings could be dramatic. The scalpel has to be used, and you have to be in control, so do not use the meat cleaver. A dollar here, and a dollar there, *all adds up!* You've fine tuned current expenses, and put them in the best possible position. Now, compare actual income with expenses, and feel good, confident, and in control. But there is a problem, **You're Short!**

Ok, Ok. I know. Relax. After all, this is *The One Hour Survival Guide for the Downsized.* It's now time to reshuffle what you have. The first and easiest strategy is to reallocate stocks, bonds, cash, and CDs to try to create a better income; a better revenue stream.

Remember, you're looking for high cash flow 1st from the asset, but liquidating the asset is not off the table.

Try to stay calm.

This too shall pass.

People don't like to live off of principal, but this is survival.

Are you living where you want to be or should be?

Since you have been downsized from your job, it may be necessary to downsize your house. Examine your surroundings. Are they really what you want? If they are, stay there. But it may be time to look at liquidating that house. Not just pulling and borrowing equity out of it through refinancing, but actually selling the house. That is traumatic. Unless you have been thinking about it I would suggest putting that strategy on the back burner. That is the action of the meat cleaver, not the scalpel.

Being downsized changes many things. That, of course, is obvious. What it shouldn't change is your being in control of your finances. Knowledge of what you have, what you need (really need), and developing a strategy to match one against the other is your initial goal of surviving being downsized.

Entertainment: We are so conditioned today to figure that our entertainment has a price tag. The bigger the price, the greater the entertainment. The reality is, that's just not so! Every community has a Weekend Guide. Check the guide! See what is happening at the parks. See what's happening at the various museums. Are there art festivals, or fairs? You would be surprised at the amount of **free** entertainment that your community offers. In fact it is usually listed on a day-by-day schedule for each month. You can probably find movies, concerts, and much more. All you have to do is look! It is entertainment that doesn't have a gigantic cost associated with it.

I have found, through the years, that discovering a good book to be one of the cheapest and most rewarding forms of entertainment. Whether it's a fast paced 'who done it' novel, a time travel to another land, or a biography of a figure who's inspired you, rediscover what reading is all about! Okay, so you haven't read a book in

Entertainment shouldn't stop ... but you may want to redefine it.

years. You've never had the time to sit down and read. Well, guess what, you've got the time now. You've been downsized, and you may discover that you've been missing an entertainment that's been there for a long time. It costs virtually nothing! A library card and a local library can help get you started. Remember, time is on your side.

Now is the time for self-control.

Clothes Shopping: So, you're used to buying the latest styles and the finest fashions. You've always been 'right on the money'. People have always said, "That guy, really looks good!", or "Boy, she's sharp!" Now, all of a sudden, an occasional blouse, shirt or pair of pants is definitely out of reach. That doesn't mean you have to stop shopping. That doesn't mean you have to stop having new clothes. You need to start to get creative. Consignment shops are popular throughout the country! People who have worn clothes for a very short period of time will send these clothes to a consignment shop. Depending upon which part of the country you live in, there are individuals who dress for a social season. Now, obviously, they have not been downsized. They were probably the 'downsizers', or the wives of the downsizer. These clothes were purchased for a particular event and never worn again. Quality merchandise including jackets, coats, blouses, shirts, pants, ties can be found in consignment shops. Here is were it gets tough! In your mind these are used goods, and somebody else's used goods are something you don't want to be associated with. Well, I don't think that's too smart, because you're looking for every dollar. They are clean, fresh, and very contemporary. Get into those stores, look for you, and for your family.

> *When my wife lost her teaching job, because of a downsizing in the district, she knew she couldn't spend money on new clothes, but she's a pretty good shopper. She chooses to buy traditional styles that never*

go out of fashion, and she looks to accessorize them.

We were visiting our daughter in Florida, in West Palm Beach, and she discovered a series of very exclusive neighborhood consignment shops. When she came home after spending a day there, she was like a kid in a candy shop! She couldn't wait to show me her discoveries! She bought a scarf, a blouse, a pin and a hat. Some with the price tags still on were reduced by 80 or 90%. I asked her the simple question, "These are goods that somebody else either wore or bought. How do you feel about that?" She looked, thought for a second; put on a hat, and said, "Doesn't this look like me?" "Yes," I said, "I see your point." She has been a frequent visitor of the consignment shops ever since!

The final revenue generator that I want to talk about I've left for last. This next strategy can be *initially* traumatic, although it has become as traditional in America as mom, apple pie, and Chevrolet. It is the yard sale. Now, I say it's traumatic because you're going to have to sell things that have been in your house for years to which you have emotional attachments. Therefore, I'm not sure that it's the way you want to go. But, there are items that are in the closet that you can't wear anymore. Let's face it, you've become more ample in your old age. But, you've held on to those old clothes just in case you started to work out. Now that you've got some time, exercise might not be a bad idea. In the event that you don't, those clothes are just hanging there. They may be more valuable to you in someone else's closet, via the local consignment shop or a yard sale. No, they may not bring the money *you* think they're going to bring, but they will help. It allows you to start to reorganize your household clutter. The extra pots, the extra pans, the extra furniture are the things that have been just sitting there that you knew you had to get rid of. Now it's time to create cash out of those items. This too is a

A yard sale?!

Are you kidding?

scalpel approach. If there is enough for a yard sale, put the signs up! Don't have them printed– that costs money! Hand letter them. You will be surprised how a few signs around the neighborhood and down the street will attract buyers like bees to honey. This is the new American phenomenon — shopping for other people's stuff. And, after all these years, you've got stuff! Have fun with it, too! It's not the end of the world. They are just inanimate objects that can raise cash. Don't let anything you're selling create an argument! If your spouse doesn't want to let it go, then *don't* sell it!

This is usually a one time shot. However, you may like this so much that you've found a whole new business! Selling other people's stuff is now called "antique dealing." But, I'm getting ahead of myself.

Do not minimize that amount of money that can be raised in a garage or yard sale!

Unemployment Compensation:
Right now there should be an overriding question that's been gnawing at the back of your mind,

> *"Well, Bill you've told me how to consolidate my assets, you've taken a look at my expenses, and my costs. I've sculpted the budget. I've looked at all the various fund raisers. I've listed the money coming in. Shouldn't I account for my unemployment compensation from the government?"*

My answer to that is...

> *Unemployment compensation, though one of the first things to apply for, is the last thing in your **mental** approach to downsizing.*

There is a reason for that!

Most people think that what they have coming from the company and their unemployment insurance are their main assets. Then they procrastinate in dealing

Don't let procrastination hinder your progress.

with everything else. I want to reverse the tables by helping you take control of your situation, by actually applying yourself to everything I've written about before. Then, when you come to the unemployment insurance, it's found money.

It's a bonus; it's icing on the cake! Trust me on this one. Stick with the budget you've established, and you'll find that this unemployment compensation is like money from Heaven.

Let's understand what unemployment compensation is all about. It is a system that is primarily funded by employers who have paid unemployment insurance taxes to the states. Is everybody eligible for unemployment insurance? Not necessarily, it all depends upon the type of job that you had, why you lost your job, whether you're able and available for other work, and your hours and wages when you were employed.

The original intention of unemployment compensation was to provide you with some financial security until you could find a job. It is a government program. When we rely on the government, we lose our initiative. We lose taking control, and this "Survival Guide" is about taking control. Oh, we'll *take* the unemployment benefits, thank you very much, because they come from tax dollars. Ultimately, they came from *our* tax dollars.

So how do you begin this process?

The process starts when you file a claim at your local unemployment benefits office. After they have received the claim, you're going to have to go through an interview process. You've been through this before with the HR Department. You're a pro. You're experienced with interviews! You're going in there; you're keeping you're cool, and you're not talking about how rotten your situation is. After all, just as the HR people had information, the unemploy-

Unemployment isn't a four-letter word

ment benefits people have some money. Granted, it may only be for 26 weeks, but it's 26 weeks that you would *very much* like to have. An interview will be scheduled, and an unemployment benefits representative will meet with you.

Before you go to the Unemployment Office, let's understand some of the basic requirements for eligibility.

The Federal Government has not mandated a national standard, and that is why the states have different eligibility requirements. There are some basics:

- You did not leave your job voluntarily without a good reason.

- You were not discharged from your job due to misconduct.

- You are able and available for work.

- You've not refused suitable work.

Of course, *none of these statements* come into play in your situation, because you've been downsized. Additionally, to be entitled to those benefits you need to have worked a certain amount of time and earned a certain amount of money. Times and amounts vary from state to state.

Many states have opted not to have an interview, and have simply gone to a form or have been automated. Additionally, if there is an interview, it could be a phone interview. Regardless, the unemployment benefits department is going to get information from you. Whether this appointment is by phone, in person, or with a questionnaire, how do you respond?

Once again, is this the place for you to spout off? The answer is, "No". You are not selling yourself. You are not telling how great an employee you are and how bad the company is. All you're giving are the facts. Joe Friday said it very well on the old Dragnet show, "Just the facts Ma'am, just the facts."

After the application has been filled out, a copy will be sent to your employer. They will have 10 days to respond to your application for benefits. In most instances, if it is a downsizing, they're not going to challenge your request. But, if they do, be prepared because you're going to have an interview about *why* your former employer is challenging your benefits.

When I first started this section, I said that I thought that this was not a basic source of income, but additional icing on the cake. The other reason I said that was because it has a limited time. In most states, you receive 26 weeks worth of unemployment benefits. You usually can collect those benefits over a 52 week period. Sometimes, if things get tough nationwide, the government can extend those benefits. Even individual states can extend beyond the 26 week time period. The extension could be for an additional 13 weeks of benefits, but after 26, 39, or whatever the set number of weeks, you don't get anything more. You don't get more, you don't get less — it ends! That is why the approach to unemployment benefits should be viewed as an additional source of income, and not the main source! It's just another one of the sources that we draw from.

Understand unemployment benefits.

For Those Denied:

Most people who have been downsized in corporate America today are not denied their unemployment benefits. For the occasional person who is, and this may come back to the fact that you are the only one being downsized, what's going to happen next? By appealing, you're going to bring your case in front of a judge or referee. You will receive an official notice in the mail. There will be an explanation as to why you were denied. That explanation may be contradictory to what you believe the case to be. When you respond to this appeal, within a specified time frame, keep your responses strictly factual. An emo-

If you don't understand what is due you... find out... ask questions.

tional response is not going to achieve anything!

Don't think this is an easy way to get money. The problem with the unemployment system is that benefits are continually monitored. Every few weeks you are going to have to respond to various questions to see if you can maintain your unemployment benefits.

- Was there work offered to you during this week?
- Did you work this week?
- Were you physically able to work full time each day of this week?

What the unemployment specialist wants to know is whether or not you're back in the workforce, or if you're scamming the government. Anytime you are dealing with government money you're jumping through hoops. That's okay, because basically that's my money, your money and other people's tax money you're getting.

We don't want it going to someone who is already back in the workforce. Therefore, the unemployment specialist monitors that very tightly.

Do you see why I kept this for last? In other areas you are in control. You don't have to answer to anybody. But with unemployment benefits you are continually responding, and you are being reminded of your situation. If we could, we might almost want to say, "Keep your money guys. It's not worth the effort!" But, we're not going to do that. We are going to get that unemployment check, and it's going to be added to everything else. We'll take it, and we'll play the game. Once again, realize that unemployment benefits have a beginning and an ending date. They don't go on forever, nor should they. It is just another one of our tools in *The One Hour Survival Guide for the Downsized.*

Unemployment is a tool. Like any tool use it well.

Emotions & Communication:

You may be starting to feel better about yourself. You may have decided that you may just be able to survive this downsizing. Congratulations, that's what you were trying to accomplish. If you have a family, they may not be at the same confidence level. Anxiety, uncertainty, and downright fear may be gripping your spouse at this moment. Partners try to put up a good front, but down deep they've been shaken. Knowing that your whole department was let go doesn't help. The statement, that it's happened to everybody, may be true, but it is not comforting to a spouse who is uncertain about *everything* at this point.

Now is really the time to work together.

The same emotions you're dealing with are the same emotions gripping your wife or husband.

Denial.

Most spouses take the attitude, Oh well, it's part of the game. Nothing has *really* changed, because they'll be back to work before you know it. Your partner thinks this kind of attitude is supportive when in reality it is *extremely* detrimental. It's detrimental because, if you buy into it, it prevents you from grabbing hold of the oars and rowing like crazy! It's the 'business as usual' syndrome. And remember, Niagara Falls is up ahead! You've been downsized. Now you understand. Your spouse must also! You can accomplish this by immediately bringing your partner into the loop.

Show your feelings! Vent! Go crazy, and then conclude by laying out your strategy. Share the plan of action, and ask if you've missed anything. Then sit down, shut up and listen to what your loved ones say. Listen to their underlying feelings and thoughts.

When only one person is rowing in a two oar row boat, you go 'round in circles!

Don't interrupt!

Don't apologize!

Don't make excuses!

Don't get confrontational!

Do keep quiet!

This is your spouse **not** the enemy, therefore.... LISTEN. The word communication is so overly used today that at times it becomes trite, but *not* in this instance. The message that must be communicated is that...

**This downsizing happened to US, and WE will get through it!
WE will survive!**

The creativity of two people working together is incredible. What you forget is that you were young once (it doesn't seem so, but you were), and you *literally* started with *nothing*. You made sacrifices, created pleasurable moments, started a family and survived to go on to greater things. Most people say, "If I could do it over...", or, "If I only knew then what I know now..." Well, you do! **You and your spouse are attacking this problem with all the love, energy AND EXPERIENCE that a lifetime together has brought!** Don't waste it. Communicate. Row together!

Children:

Children know what's going on. If you think they don't, then your ship has just arrived from another planet. They watch TV, surf the net, and talk to friends. They know what is happening. Their denial is usually one of, it's not my problem, it's my father's or mother's. It's not going to affect me. That kind of thinking has to be changed, but not with the proverbial meat cleaver.

It takes time to explain what's happened, why it happened and what your plan of action is to survive. This conversation

You're not fooling the kids.

with the children must be done with a united front. It must be presented by you and your spouse, so don't schedule the meeting until the two of you have your act together. But, don't dawdle or procrastinate, because your kids can be allies in your battle for survival. They can also be a big pain if they are uninformed. Explain that the strategies are not set in stone, and that any ideas they have are most welcome. If the ideas have merit, they will be used.

**All of a sudden, we have more oars rowing the boat!
Good bye, Niagara Falls!**

Let the kids know there will be periodic meetings to go over the situation, and receive their suggestions in addition to their thoughts. Every family member must be brought into the loop! There will be times, however, that you'll need to let off some steam, express your fears and concerns, or just cry. Don't be afraid to lean on that buddy that you've been there for, or a co-worker going through the same situation, or even a sibling. Now it's your turn, but be careful not to overuse these people. You may find that, as sensitive as they are to your situation, continually hearing about you gets old. Pick your spots, and pick their brains! Maybe they have an idea or two to implement into your survival strategy for being downsized. Don't be afraid to ask others for their thoughts! Take all the information you can get.

Other Sources:

Various churches, community centers and corporate support groups have developed resources for you to utilize. Check around with co-workers, family, friends and even your old company (yes, that too) as to what's out there and who's available.

Meeting on a periodic basis with others in your predicament *may be* of help. I say "may be", because there are many who have chosen not to start rowing. I really don't want you associated with them. You'll know after the first meeting whether or not it will add to your survival strategy. If it doesn't, you're history, you're out of there, sayonara, good bye. We will now only associate with *positive* people with action plans.

Don't overlook the Internet.

Sometimes the Internet can be an informational source. I tend to stay away from chat rooms and chat groups. You don't know who is on the other end. You don't know the accuracy of the information being supplied. You want to be able to look at the other person you contact eyeball to eyeball. So, be careful when you deal with the Internet.

Some will recommend professional counseling. Assistance from career counselors or recruiters is okay as long as it's free. I strongly believe that an action plan that you have created eliminates the need for professional counseling.

Okay, since you bought this book and paid me I will give you the only feel good professional counseling you'll need.

**You've been downsized.
It's not your fault!
Get over it! Start rowing!**

Okay, are you happy? That wasn't a long session. You didn't have to come to my office, and you didn't have to lie on a couch! Enough of the dependency talk. Emotional well being is not a subject to be taken lightly. Everyone is going to react differently to being downsized. I can't tell you how *you'll* react, but I can tell you that this response should be universal.

**I am in control. I have a plan.
I have a family that knows all.
We will survive!**

Coordination of Professionals:

You've been downsized. You had your HR meeting and it went well. You received all the information that you were looking for. You've laid out a game plan that makes sense. It will create a cash flow that will allow you to maintain a lifestyle that you're comfortable with. You've had various discussions with your partner and other members of your family. It would appear you're all on the same wave length. How can you be certain that you didn't miss something in the strategy you have designed? Perhaps you over looked an item that will create a better opportunity. Who knows? There may be a better way. Then again, you may have put together the nearly perfect (because nobody is perfect) plan. Confirmation is necessary, and that means consulting with a professional.

Here is where it gets tricky. A lot of, so called, "professionals" are lurking in the weeds simply biding their time waiting to sell you something. You may just be buying their hourly rate, so let's examine who would be appropriate to consult. I've said that I would give $100 to any person who could tell me that their broker, attorney, accountant, financial advisor, insurance agent and Rabbi, priest or minister have come together to discuss their financial situation and develop a plan. My $100 has been safe for many years. This collaborative process just doesn't happen. All of these individuals are approaching you from different disciplines, with different vested interests. Under normal circumstances, you would be the coordinator — the quarterback — in organizing some cohesion between this group. Remember, if it doesn't happen naturally it's certainly not going to happen now that you've been DOWNSIZED. In the event that you do find someone, or a firm that can wear several hats, you are fortunate. Much of the battle for coordinated information has been won! (Eagle Steward Ltd., the firm that I founded over a decade ago, was designed with exactly that approach in mind. Check out the website:

A good place to start:

www. eaglesteward. com.

www.eaglesteward.com.) Let's examine the interests of broker, registered rep, financial consultant or financial planner.

They used to call them "customer's men" — which is an interesting title. They will be happy to talk with you when they hear you have a 401(k) to work with. Before you make an appointment, ask a few questions, such as:

- How long have you been in the business?
- Do you have any credentials?
- What is your area of concentration?
- How are you compensated?
- Can you supply any references for the past three years?

There are probably many other questions you can ask. However, these seem to be the core. Explain carefully that you've been downsized, that you've laid out a game plan, and that you would like to review it with them. Ask if there is any cost for the initial meeting. There should be no cost. However, if there is, reevaluate the person and look elsewhere.

How do you find this person in the first place? Ask former colleagues, neighbors, friends or relatives. Look at TV, newspaper or listen to radio. Some of the better financial people like to share their knowledge and experience through these media. They also think it's good advertising. Get two or three names and then go to work with your call and inquiries.

I've dwelt on the financial people for good reason. Although attorneys and accountants are specialists, the conversation with them is certain to cost an hourly rate. Remember every dollar of cost adds up! And more importantly, in most instances the attorney and/or accountant is not licensed to give financial advice. Unfortunately today, both professions have a tendency of stepping over the line when it comes to giving financial information. I suggest you stick with the folks who do financial work — construction and reconstruction on a daily basis. Try to keep your advisors to a minimum. Remember, the more you have the more you'll receive well intentioned but conflicting advice. I prefer to stick with only **one**.

Meeting with the Advisor:

Be ready! Don't waste their time with a sad story about your situation. Besides, there is no sad story. Yes, you've been downsized, but now you are in control. Explain your situation to the advisor. Lay out your assets, liabilities and cash flow. Demonstrate the strategy that you think is best for you, and then once again *be quiet*. Listen to what the planner has to say. I'm sure you'll be asked several questions including, "Is this the end of the line, or are you going to go back into the workforce?" I will address this question in the last two sections. For now, what you're looking for is confirmation that your strategy will allow you, your partner, and your family to survive.

Perhaps a paid advisor is really the best move you can make.

Be open minded! Just because you laid out the strategy doesn't mean that it can't be tweaked a little or dramatically improved. If the advisor casually scans the plan and says, "Yep, looks good to me." Pick up your papers, say, "Thank you", and leave. You are not looking for someone who treats you lightly. This is serious stuff. It's your survival! What you are looking for is someone who has a brain, will take time to understand your situation, and show empathy. Sometimes all these are not easy to find, but don't settle for less! The advisor may state that the time required to analyze your total situation will require a fee. Don't be afraid. Get a quote, and make your judgment accordingly. The advisor may be the best thing since sliced bread. All along the way I've urged you to take control. You can remain in control even when consulting with a professional for confirmation and/or advice. You've not abdicated your position. A professional is just another tool that you'll use in *The One Hour Survival Guide for the Downsized.*

Back to Work:

The first reaction to being downsized is normally to declare to yourself that this is only temporary and that another job is waiting right around the corner. This is a detrimental denial. I've watched people who for years continue to wait for the exact same job they just left, and continue to wait, and continue to wait. Believe it or not this reaction can be revamped to create new possibilities.

You were just downsized. The job you had, the job that you developed, that you in essence created is gone. The exact job is no more. But there is another one waiting, if you want it.

So what do you do first? Well, here we go with lists again. Remember when I told you to list all your assets to get a handle on what you've accumulated over your lifetime. Now I want you to make a list of all

Take a skills inventory.

your skills that you've developed since you've been on this planet.

I don't differentiate, blue collar or white collar work, that would be too limiting. What I want is a list of what you *like* to do coupled with what you feel you are *good* at. It may be a simple thing like stripping and repairing a car engine. Think about your skills, traits, and positive qualities. I want you to develop this list because everything on this list is a potential job category, and within those categories are several jobs.

Sample List: outgoing, like to talk, enjoy children, meet people easily, like early mornings, patient, love to golf, fish, NASCAR, read, ...

Now with this list place a potential job next to it. By the way, put down every potential job that you can think of, no matter how outlandish (ex: NASCAR — pit crew). By the way, if you've gotten creative, this list could go on for several pages. If it doesn't, you haven't looked at

As much as the phrase gets on peoples' nerves — now is the time to think outside the box.

all of your qualities, or your likes. Ask your partner to help by describing you to yourself. Sometimes this is dangerous (just kidding), but it could add several more potential jobs to your list. Now that you have a list of potential jobs set it aside. Let's go back to the normal-next step that everyone does, and you will too. Checking out your field or expertise.

Examine the area where you live. Companies that compete with your former employer may be in the hiring mode. It would not hurt to examine the neighborhood.

Now, I define neighborhood as 'the world at large', because your profession may have openings, but they could be 2000 miles away. This then becomes a totally different decision, one of uprooting yourself and family to a completely different part of the country. If it is just you that is not so bad, but if it's an entire family the negatives may out weigh the job itself. This discussion I'll leave to others as I'm just concerned with your survival.

This is the traditional attempt of trying to stay in the same profession that you've been in all your life. This is the natural reaction in looking for another job. However, I put it second, because I wanted you to first see all the potential jobs that were available. It suggests that your next job is only limited by you and what you want to do. What I want you to understand is that **you do not have to be a slave to your profession.**

This may be a good point to insert the three things you'll need to get your next job. The first is your résumé . Next is your understanding of the new job and what you can bring to the new employer, and finally, is your presentation of self.

Résumé Time.

The Résumé — If you have the Internet, search for examples of résumé writing. I don't want to re-create the wheel, because they do such a good job. If you don't have Internet access go to a library which does have Internet access. Ask the librarian for help! It should be free (another way to save money). Professional résumé writers are a possibility, but the expense may be prohibitive.

Understanding the New Job and What You Can Bring to It — This is crucial, not only in your interview, but also for other potential employers. Make sure you've researched exactly what the company's goals and objectives are. Learn their history, the successes and failures, and picture yourself on their team. Understand what you mean to them. Remember, central to surviving being downsized is control and knowledge of self. To go back into the workplace you must have as much information about a potential employer as you can find. This gives you the advantage in survival!!!

Presentation of Self — Before you are scheduled for your job interview, check out how the employees are attired. If they are in shirts and ties, then you show up in a shirt and tie. If they are dressed business casual, then you should be in business casual. Be punctual. That means be there ahead of schedule. Allow for all delays; don't be late.

Now for a little trick. When you get to the interview listen to what the interviewer is asking and saying, and keep your mind open. Remember there are *no* right or wrong answers in an interview. They are trying to get to know you. The trick is called facing.

When the interviewer leans forward, you lean forward (shows your interest). When the interviewer sits back, you sit back (shows you're relaxed). Don't mix that up!! We don't want you being casual when the interviewer is intense, and vise versa.

I realize I've given you some interview tips and you're probably wondering, "where does this interview come from?" The job can be listed in many areas: the newspaper, magazines, the Internet, at your local church, at meeting halls and even by word mouth. Keep your eyes and

How long has it been since you've been interviewed.

ears open, and don't be afraid to ask people you see about who is hiring.

Sitting back and waiting for someone to call you is popular, safe and very, very unproductive. You have to find every potential employer in your field, and know exactly what their current hiring situation is. This effort will take time. But, once again that's what you have — time, because you've been downsized.

I said earlier NOT to be a slave to your profession. So, what if there are absolutely no jobs for you in your field? Regardless, if there are longer hours or lower pay and there is nothing that you see that you want, don't panic. In fact, I want you to start to feel in control, because I'm not even sure you wanted to stay in the same field.

You see, we're financially O.K. We've compiled our lists, did our analysis and determined that we don't really need the same income to survive. Now it's a question of choice. So let's go back to our first group of lists about our likes and our personality traits. You've discovered that you have two overriding loves, besides your family. The first is cooking. Your cheese omelets are the best, and your chocolate cake is the envy of every housewife in the neighborhood. The next passion is tinkering with old cars. You love getting under the hood of a '57 Chevy, and making that engine just hum. These are just two examples. You can probably find many others.

Now revisit the newspaper, magazines, Internet, local church, meeting hall and even casual conversation (sound familiar), but this time you're looking for other jobs. You're now looking for the kind of work you really would like to do.

There is a problem, however, and that is experience. You have none when it comes to this new job. But you have something that your competitors don't have — a youthful enthusiasm (remember this is all new) and a desire to succeed that you've probably not felt in a long time.

The new job may take more education, more learning, after all you probably shouldn't expect to start as the executive chef at the Waldorf, or as the chief mechanic in a NASCAR pit crew right away. But, remember the fact is that your talent and enthusiasm will be recognized. **Real** talent and **real** enthusiasm will be rewarded.

I just mentioned money. Let's face it, starting again in another profession, another career, is not going to be financially rewarding immediately. But, that's okay, because all we're looking to do *immediately* is *survive*. The money will come later.

It may be difficult to believe — but this may not be a catastrophe. It could be a real opportunity!

Bernie thought what a difference there was from making decisions about product placement at Kodak over 32 years to making sure the parsley looked fresh when he placed it on the entree plate. He was going to meet Cheryl for a glass of wine, but that wasn't for another two hours. Imagine, top Eastman Kodak Executive, downsized, Burger King, short order cook school, and now assistant to the Head Chef in the hottest restaurant in Boca. "I love this," he said smiling as he pushed dinner plates out to anxious waiters. "What did you say Bernie," Paul asked. "Nothing, nothing at all," Bernie said. Downsizing seemed a long way off.

A new career, a new job, excitement, the unknown... You're probably wondering, "why didn't this happen to me long ago? Look at the time I've wasted!" No you haven't. It took downsizing for you to wake up and realize all of your opportunities.

SECTION THREE

Opportunities Come in Different Forms

OPPORTUNITIES CAN COME in different forms, sizes and shapes. The fact that you were downsized has finally sunk in. This is not a catastrophe, but an opportunity.

THE ONE HOUR SURVIVAL GUIDE

But to do what????

My Definition of Retirement is ...

having the financial where-with-all to do exactly what you want to do.

The power of positive attitude cannot be overstated.

Having completed your financial checklist, your assets versus liabilities, and income versus expenses, you may find that you have reached the point in your life when you qualify for the definition that I just gave you. This could present a very major psychological challenge. First of all, you've been downsized. The company you've worked for all these years has said goodbye. That, as we've seen, presents its own problems, but the real difficulty is facing the fact that you've discovered, or have been told by a professional, that **you don't have to work if you don't want to....You don't need the money!!!**

Many of you are saying, "I wish that was me. What's he talking about? I know exactly what to do." Oh, really! Would you?

Positive attitude can do more than most people realize.

Encourage it and maintain it.

You're now retired. You can do whatever it is you want to do, within your finances, of course. ***But***, the problem is we are all conditioned to have some form or structure; at the job by 8 o' clock, lunch around noon, leave by 5 o'clock, overtime every Tuesday and Thursday, two weeks of vacation, and on, and on.... You get the point. We are conditioned. When we've been downsized the shock of taking us out of our routine is offset, because it's someone else's decision. ***But***, when it becomes our decision to retire, our psyche has a very difficult time adapting and complying.

Once the shock has worn off, and you realize that what you do each morning is totally in your hands, you will feel a freedom that you never thought existed. The choice of working or not working, volunteering or not volunteering, traveling or not traveling, even getting up or staying in bed is totally yours.

What you'll soon discover, so I'm told, is that you won't know how you ever found the time to work. You'll be echoing the retiree's lament: Not enough time, not enough time.

Imagine that just a short time ago you were totally devastated by the thought of being downsized. Now you thank God that it happened.

Enjoy— You earned it!

The power to control your situation and the power to control your attitude are what we are ultimately trying to achieve. No one can do it for you. No group, book, TV show or video can replace the power that lies within you to achieve your goals.

SECTION FOUR

Further Reading

THERE ARE THREE BOOKS that I would urge you to acquire then read again, and again, and again (check the library, it's cheaper).

The first is *The Millionaire Next Door: The Surprising Secrets of America's Wealthy* by Thomas J. Stanley and William Danko. What you will learn is that from the humblest beginnings various individuals, just like you, amassed a wealth that even they thought was beyond them. They did it by organizing themselves and being disciplined in their approach to life.

Neither the authors or I can tell you what is right for you, but we can, and I have, suggested strategies to take you from the depth of despair about being downsized to the heights of ecstasy about achieving control.

The next book was written many years ago, but continues to be a best seller. I sincerely believe it is one of two cornerstones in all motivational speakers programs. *Think and Grow Rich* by Napoleon Hill will teach the specifics of your goals.

When you have decided the kind of job you want, if you are reentering the work force, Hill's book will teach you that by setting the specific goal (ex: the exact job) your subconscious will continually force you to come up with ways to put yourself in the position for acquiring that new job. If it's survival for the next month, you will learn that setting specific goals and objectives are much more successful that those that are generalized.

Examples:
"I want to work again"
vs.
"I want to be a cook in a large camp with children"
"I want to go out for an evening"
vs.
"I want to see a play and have a meal all for under $30"

Get specific! Challenge your conscious *and* your sub-conscious.

The third book I want you to *own*, that's right, *own*, not *borrow* is the *Bible*. It is irrelevant to me what religion you are. What I want you to realize is that God has dealt with all of the emotions that you are experiencing right now. Stress to Him is nothing new. Neither is money, a job, a family, or anything else that is troubling you right now. Every problem conceivable is addressed in the Bible. If you haven't looked at it as a reference guide, then you've missed the whole point of what it's all about. Whether you are a believer or not, and for your sake I hope you are, God's answers are for everyone.

Absorbing what you've learned about you and your situation, understanding through *The Millionaire Next Door* that you can achieve your goals, identifying your goals with *Think and Grow Rich*, and finally, ***The One Hour Survival Guide for the Downsized*** tells you that you can be in control of the process. When all these references are combined with Biblical principles, you will experience a level of success that neither one of us could ever have imagined.

CONCLUSION

THIS BOOK WAS NOT WRITTEN as a step by step hand held guide for you. It was not written for me to give you all the answers. As a matter of fact, many of the chapters simply touch the tip of the iceberg as it pertains to that area. If I had written your game plan, you would now be my client. Because you are an individual, no self help book can know exactly who you are, what you're going through, or how you feel.

What I hope you understand is that being downsized was not your decision, but what happens *now* certainly is. You have the intelligence, the experience, the guts, and now, the know how to take what appears to be a bad situation and turn it into a good opportunity. Getting from that first moment of learning you've been downsized to the moment you realize everything will be all right is up to you — only you and no one else.

I hope I've had a small hand in your survival.

APPENDIX

Lists

WILLIAM L. TATRO, IV

NON QUALIFIED, PERSONAL & QUALIFIED ASSETS
(LIST #1)

Non Qualified Assets:

Name or Description	Current Account Value	Current Rate of Return	Cost Basis	Ownership (ie. Client, Spouse, JTWROS, JTTEN, Trust)
CASH, checking	$			
CASH, savings	$			
CASH, CD'S Maturity Dates:	$			
MONEY MARKET	$			
SAVINGS BONDS	$			
U.S. TREASURIES Bonds, Notes, T-Bills	$			
TAXABLE BONDS	$			
MUNICIPAL BONDS	$			
ANNUITIES	$			
NOTES/MORTGAGES (receivable)	$			
MUTUAL FUNDS:				
BOND	$			
STOCK	$			
STOCKS	$			

THE ONE HOUR SURVIVAL GUIDE

NON QUALIFIED, PERSONAL & QUALIFIED ASSETS
LIST #1 Continued

Non Qualified Assets:

Name or Description	Current Account Value	Current Rate of Return	Cost Basis	Ownership (ie. Client, Spouse, JTWROS, JTTEN, Trust)
REAL ESTATE (Investment Properties Only) Describe:	$			
LTD. PARTNERSHIPS Describe:	$			
OTHER	$			

Insurance Policy Information:

Description	Client Amount	Spouse Amount
Nursing Home/Home Care **Current Cash Value**	$	$
Employer Disability **Current Cash Value**	$	$
Employer Group-Term Life **Current Cash Value**	$	$
Personal Life Insurance **Current Cash Value**	$	$

WILLIAM L. TATRO, IV

NON QUALIFIED, PERSONAL & QUALIFIED ASSETS
LIST #1 Continued

Personal Assets:

Current Fair Market Value

Primary Residence $_____

Vacation Residence $_____

Personal Property $_____   Please note that these
includes   numbers should be market
home furnishings,   values, NOT replacement
appliances   cost!

Art $_____

Jewelry $_____

Collections $_____   Describe:_____
e.g. Stamp, Coin

Automobiles $_____   Year:_____   Car Name:_____
   $_____   Year:_____   Car Name:_____

Boats, RV's $_____   Describe:_____

THE ONE HOUR SURVIVAL GUIDE

NON QUALIFIED, PERSONAL & QUALIFIED ASSETS
LIST #1 Continued

Qualified Assets:

	YOUR'S		SPOUSE	
	Current Account Value	Current Rate of Return	Current Account Value	Current Rate of Return
Description				
403B / TSA	$		$	
PROFIT - SHARING	$		$	
401K PLAN*	$		$	
DEFERRED COMP*.	$		$	
KEOGH*	$		$	
SEP*	$		$	
IRA'S*	$		$	
ROTH IRA'S*	$		$	

*List Sub Accounts
& Values if Appropriate

PERSONAL LIABILITIES
LIST #2

Mortgages:

Description	Current Mortgage Principal	Monthly Prin./Int. Payment	Current Interest Rate
Primary Residence	$	$	%
Vacation Residence	$	$	%

Non-Mortgage Liabilities:

Description	Outstanding Balance	Monthly Payment	Interest Rate
Home Equity Loan	$	$	%
Auto Loan	$	$	%
Credit Card Debt	$	$	%
Other Loans (ex: from an insurance policy) Describe:	$	$	%

THE ONE HOUR SURVIVAL GUIDE

INCOME
LIST #3

	YOUR'S	SPOUSE
If collecting **severance pay** income: Current monthly severance pay income Source: _____	$	$
If NOT receiving severance pay income: Estimated monthly severance pay income Source: _____	$	$
If collecting **vacation pay** reimbursements: Current monthly vacation pay income Source: _____	$	$
If NOT receiving vacation pay reimbursements: Estimated monthly vacation pay income Source: _____	$	$
If collecting **sick day** reimbursements: Current monthly sick day income Source: _____	$	$
If NOT sick day reimbursements: Estimated monthly sick day income Source: _____	$	$
If collecting **rental property** income: Current monthly rental income Source: _____	$	$

INCOME
LIST #3 Continued

	YOUR'S	SPOUSE
If NOT receiving rental property income: Estimated monthly rental income Source: _____	$	$
If collecting income from a friendly loan: Current monthly amount repaid Source: _____	$	$
If NOT receiving income **from a friendly loan**: Estimated monthly amount to be repaid Source: _____	$	$
If collecting **retirement income**: Current monthly pension income Source: _____	$	$
If NOT receiving retirement income: Estimated monthly pension income	$	$
If collecting **social security benefits**: Current monthly social security check	$	$
If NOT collecting social security now: Estimated monthly social security check	$	$
Age at which you expect to start receiving social security benefits		

THE ONE HOUR SURVIVAL GUIDE

INCOME

LIST #3 Continued

Insurance \ Annuity Policy Income Information:

Description	Your Amount	Spouse Amount
Nursing Home/Home Care **Monthly Benefit**	$	$
Employer Disability **Monthly Benefit**	$	$
Annuity Contracts **Monthly Benefit**	$	$

WILLIAM L. TATRO, IV

PERSONAL BUDGET EXPENDITURES
LIST #4

Description of Expenditure	Monthly OR Amount	Annual Amount
RENT, Apartment, etc.	$	$
LEASING, Automobile	$	$
FOOD, And Household Expenses	$	$
GAS, ELECTRIC, WATER	$	$
TELEPHONE	$	$
AUTO, Gas Oil, Repairs, Maint.	$	$
CLOTHING, & Personal Items	$	$
PROPERTY IMPROVEMENTS	$	$
REAL ESTATE TAXES	$	$
CHARITABLE CONTRIBUTIONS	$	$
ENTERTAINMENT	$	$
VACATIONS	$	$
HOME FURNISHINGS	$	$

THE ONE HOUR SURVIVAL GUIDE

PERSONAL BUDGET EXPENDITURES
LIST #4 Continued

Description of Expenditure	Monthly OR Amount	Annual Amount
SUBSCRIPTIONS	$	$
GIFTS, Birthdays, Christmas, etc.	$	$
MEDICAL/DENTAL, Unreimbursed	$	$
DOMESTIC HELP/CHILD CARE	$	$
INSURANCE PREMIUMS TOTAL	$	$

Nursing Home Ins. Premiums
Disability Insurance Premiums
Life Insurance Premiums
Company Group-Term
Personal Life
Auto Insurance Premiums
Homeowner's Insurance Premiums
Medical/Dental Ins. Premiums
Medicare Insurance Premiums

| OTHER: | $ | $ |

WILLIAM L. TATRO, IV

PERSONAL FINANCIAL COMPARISON
LIST #5

TOTAL MONEY INCOMING	TOTAL MONEY OUT-GOING
$_____	$_____
$_____	$_____
$_____	$_____
$_____	$_____
$_____	$_____
$_____	$_____
$_____	$_____
$_____	$_____
$_____	$_____
$_____	$_____
$_____	$_____
$_____	$_____
$_____	$_____
$_____	$_____
$_____	$_____
$_____	$_____
$_____ **TOTALS**	$_____

APPENDIX

Notes

Notes

WILLIAM L. TATRO IV

Notes

THE ONE HOUR SURVIVAL GUIDE
Notes

WILLIAM L. TATRO IV

Notes

THE ONE HOUR SURVIVAL GUIDE
Notes

WILLIAM L. TATRO IV

Notes

THE ONE HOUR SURVIVAL GUIDE
Notes

WILLIAM L. TATRO IV

Notes

THE ONE HOUR SURVIVAL GUIDE
Notes